Out of the Blue

Simon Armitage
Out of the Blue

ENITHARMON PRESS

First published in 2008
by Enitharmon Press
26B Caversham Road
London NW5 2DU

www.enitharmon.co.uk

Distributed in the UK by
Central Books
99 Wallis Road
London E9 5LN

Distributed in the USA and Canada
by Dufour Editions Inc.
PO Box 7, Chester Springs
PA 19425, USA

ISBN: 978-1-904634-58-4 (paperback)
ISBN: 978-1-904634-59-1 (signed limited edition, hardback)

Enitharmon Press gratefully acknowledges the financial support of
Arts Council England, London.

British Library Cataloguing-in-Publication Data.
A catalogue record for this book is available
from the British Library.

Designed by Libanus Press
and printed in England by
Antony Rowe Ltd

CONTENTS

ACKNOWLEDGEMENTS

Out of the Blue was a Silver River production for Five, and was directed by Ned Williams. *We May Allow Ourselves a Brief Period of Rejoicing* was a talkbackTHAMES production for Five and was also directed by Ned Williams. The poem *Cambodia* was commissioned by BBC Radio 3 as part of the programme *The Violence of Silence,* and was directed by Kate Rowland. Many thanks to all those involved.

Out of the Blue

1

All lost.
All lost in the dust.
Lost in the fall and the crush and the dark.
Now all coming back.

2

Up with the lark, downtown New York.
The sidewalks, the blocks.
Walk. Don't Walk. Walk. Don't Walk.

Breakfast to go:
an adrenalin shot
in a Styrofoam cup.

Then plucked from the earth,
rocketed skyward,
a fifth of a mile

in a minute, if that.
The body arrives,
the soul catches up.

3

That weird buzz
of being at work
in the hour before work.

All terminals dormant,
all networks idle.
Systems in sleep-mode,

all stations un-peopled.
I get here early
just to gawp from the window.

Is it shameless or brash to have reached the top,
just me and America
ninety floors up?

Is it brazen to feel like a king, like a God,
to be surfing the wave
of a power trip,

a fortune under each fingertip,
a billion a minute, a million a blink,
selling sand to the desert,

ice to the Arctic,
money to the rich.
The elation of trading in futures and risk.

Here I stand, a compass needle,
a sundial spindle
right at the pinnacle.

Under my feet
Manhattan's a simple bagatelle, a pinball table,
all lights and mirrors and whistles and bells.

The day begun.
The sun like a peach.
A peach of a sun.

And everything framed
by a seascape dotted with ferries and sails
and a blue sky zippered with vapour trails.

Beyond this window
it's vast and it's sheer.
Exhilaration. All breath. All clear.

4

Arranged on the desk
among rubber bands and bulldog clips:

here is a rock from Brighton beach,
here is a beer-mat, here is the leaf

of an oak, pressed and dried, papery thin.
Here is a Liquorice Allsorts tin.

A map of the Underground pinned to the wall.
The flag of St George. A cricket ball.

Here is calendar, counting the days.
Here is a photograph snug in its frame:

this is my wife on our wedding day,
here is a twist of her English hair.

Here is a picture in purple paint:
two powder-paint towers, heading for space,

plus rockets and stars and the Milky Way,
plus helicopters and aeroplanes.

Jelly-copters and fairy-planes.
In a spidery hand, underneath it, it says,

'If I stand on my toes can you see me wave?'

5

The towers at one.
The silent prongs of a tuning fork,
testing the calm.

Then a shudder or bump.
A juddering thump or a thud.
I swear no more

than a thump or a thud.
But a Pepsi Max jumps out of its cup.
And a filing cabinet spews its lunch.

And the water-cooler staggers then slumps.
Then a sonic boom and the screen goes blue.
Then a deep, ungodly dragon's roar.

Then ceiling tiles, all awry at once,
and a soft, white dust snowing down from above.
See, there in the roof,

the cables, wires, pipes and ducts,
the veins and fibres and nerves and guts,
exposed and unstrung.

In their shafts, the lift-cars clang
and the cables are plucked:
a deep, sub-human, inaudible twang.

And a lurch.
A pitch.
A sway to the south.

I know for a fact these towers can stand
the shoulder-charge of a gale force wind
or the body-check of hurricane.

But this is a punch, a hammer-blow.
I sense it thundering underfoot,
a pulsing, burrowing, aftershock,

down through the bone-work of girders and struts,
down into earth and rock.
Right to the root.

The horizon totters and lists.
The line of the land seems to teeter
on pins and stilts,

a perceptible tilt.
Then the world re-aligns, corrects itself.
Then hell lets loose.

And I know we are torn.
I know we are holed
because through that hole

a torrent of letters and memos and forms
now streams and storms
now flocks and shoals
now passes and pours
now tacks and jibes
now flashes and flares
now rushes and rides
now flaps and glides ...

the centrefold of the *New York Times*
goes winging by

then a lamp
a coat
a screen
a chair

a yoghurt pot
a yucca plant
a yellow cup
a Yankees cap.

A shoe, freeze-framed against the open sky.
I see raining flames.
I see hardware fly.

6

Millicent wants an answer now.
Anthony talks through a megaphone.
Mitch says it looks like one of those days.
Abdoul calls his mother at home.

Christopher weeps for his cat and his dog.
Monica raises her hand to her eye.
Lee goes by with his arm on fire.
Abigail opens a bottom drawer.

Raymond punches a hole in the wall.
Pedro loosens his collar and tie.
Ralph and Craig join an orderly queue.
Amy goes back to look for her purse .

Joseph presses his face to the glass.
Theresa refrains from raising her voice.
Abdoul tries his mother again.
Bill pulls a flashlight out of his case.

Tom replaces the top of a pen.
Peter hears voices behind the door.
Abdoul tries his mother again.
Glen writes a note on a paper plane.

Gloria's plan is another dead-end.
Paul draws a scarf over Rosemary's face.
Arnold remembers the name of his wife.
Judy is looking for Kerry and Jack.

Edwardo lights a cigarette.
Dennis goes down on his hands and knees.
Stephanie edges out onto the ledge.
Jeremy forces the door of the lift.

Ethan gets married in less than a month.
Kwame is struggling under the weight.
Connie won't leave without locking her desk.
Mike lifts a coat-stand over his head.

Elaine is making a call to a school.
Claude won't be needing this any more.
Rosa and Bob never stood a chance.
Josh goes looking but doesn't come back.

7

Go up go down. Sit tight for now. Or move. Don't move. It's all in hand. Make a call on the phone. Stay calm. Then shout. Stay calm. Then SHOUT. Come back. I think we should leave but not in the lift. This staircase closed. This stairwell black. Keep cool. Keep your head. For fuck's sake man this telephone's dead. Get low to the floor. Who bolted this door? Try the key, try the code. Hit nine one one. Come away from the glass. Keep back from the heat. Heat rises, right? Go down. Go south. That exit locked. That lobby blocked. That connecting corridor clogged with stone. The lights go out. Come on. Go out. A fire alarm drones. Come away from the edge. Hit nine one one. Come here and see, we made the news. Try CNN. Try ABC. They say it's a plane. So bung it with something to stop the smoke. Or we choke. Use a skirt, use a shirt. Rescue services now on their way. What with? With what – with a magic carpet? A thousand foot rope? Stand back form the door. They're saying it's war. Don't break the glass – don't fan the flames. Outside it's air. Outside it's sheer. A wing and a prayer. Go up. Go north. Get out on the roof. No way. Call home. It's daddy, ask mummy to come to the phone. Get mummy, tell mummy to come to the phone. Just DO AS YOU'RE TOLD. This glass, like metal. If we step out there . . . if we stay in here. This glass, like metal. Just DO AS YOU'RE TOLD. Get mummy, tell mummy to come to the phone. It's daddy, ask mummy to come to the phone. Call home. No way. Get out on the roof. Go north. Go up. A wing and a prayer. Outside it's sheer. Outside it's air. Don't break the glass – don't fan the flames. They're saying it's war. Stand back from the door. With what – a magic carpet? What with? A thousand foot rope. Rescue services now on their way. Use a skirt, use a shirt. Or we choke. So bung it with something to stop the smoke. They say it's a plane. Try ABC. Try CNN. Come here and see, we made the news. Hit nine one one. Come away from the edge. A fire alarm drones. Go out. Come on. The lights go out. That connecting corridor clogged with stone. That lobby blocked. That exit locked. Go south. Go down. Heat rises, right? Keep back from the heat. Come away from the glass. Hit nine one one. Try the key, try the code. Who bolted this door? Get low to the floor. For fuck's sake man this telephone's dead. Keep your head. Keep cool. This stairwell black. This staircase closed. I think we should leave but not in the lift. Come back. Then SHOUT. Stay calm. Then shout. Stay calm. Make a call on the phone. It's all in hand. Don't move. Or move. Sit tight for now. Go up go down. Sit tight for now. Go up. Go down.

8

Fire as a rumour at first.
Fire as a whisper of wolves,
massing and howling

beneath the floor,
clawing and scrabbling,
tongues of flame licking under the door.

And smoke like fear.
Smoke as a bear, immense and barrelling,
horribly near.

Then furious heat.
Incensed.
Every atom irate and alive with heat.

And air won't arrive.
Un-breathed, an ocean of sky
goes sailing past on the other side.

Now heat with its nails in your eye.
With its breath in your face.
With its hands in your hair,

its fist in your throat.
So the window shatters,
the glass goes through.

Crane into the void.
Lean into the world.
It's not in my blood

to actually jump.
I don't have the juice.
But others can't hold.

So a body will fall. And a body will fall.
And a body will fall. And a body will fall.
A body will drop

through the faraway hole
of vanishing point,
smaller then gone,

till the distant hit and the burst of dust.
The shock. The stain
of fruit and stone.

9

I was fighting for breath.
I was pounding the glass
when a shape flew past . . .

A snapshot only.
The shape of a cross, as it were.
Just a blur.

But detail. Fact.
An engine. A wing.
I sort of swayed, sort of thing,

sort of swooned, that fear
when something designed to be far
comes illogically near.

Then it banked. It scooped. It was tipping.
Not dipping away
but towards.

Then the groan and the strain
as it turned.
I see it now, over and over,

frame by frame by frame.
Then everything burned.
And I thought – how crazy is this –

this can't be the case.
I actually thought there's got to be some mistake:
they'll wind back the film,

call back the plane,
they'll try this again.
The day will be fine,

put back as it was. This time they'll steer!
Because lightning never strikes once,
let alone twice,

and no two planes just happened to veer
through mechanical fault
or human error,

one after the other.
It must be a mirage.
It must be mirror.

That thought didn't last.
That thought was a lie
which darkened and died the second it formed.

Then it dawned.
What else is a plane but a flying bomb?
A man with his arm in his hand, in a mess, mumbles
    'this is so wrong.'

10

We are spinning a web.
We are knotting a net.
These are delicate threads.

These are desperate times.
We are throwing out lines
so subtle and slight

they are lighter than air.
We are spanning the sky
with wireless wires

too faint by far
for the naked eye,
untraceably thin, imperceptibly fine.

But they carry our breath.
We are making our calls.
These are tightropes, strung

from the end of the phone
to a place called home
so our words can escape,

our voices trapeze
for mile after mile
or in my case traverse

the width of the sea.
My beautiful wife,
sit down in the chair,

put the phone to your ear.
Let me say.
Let me hear.

We are spinning a web.
Such delicate threads,
the links so brittle,

too little, too late.
Not one can save us
or bear our weight.

11

Then enormity falls.
Then all sense fails.

The strings are cut
and the world goes slack.

The tower to the south,
holding on to the moon by its fingernails

now loses its fix
and drops from view.

The tower to the south
now loses heart,

now sieves itself through itself.
Just gives up the ghost.

All logic and fact on the slide.
Through a crack in the sky

for a second or so . . .
a river . . . and land on the other side.

Then the image lost
to uplift of ash and an inrush of dust.

Then the overwhelming urge to run.
The impulse to pump with the arms and fists,

sprint hell-for-leather up seventh or fifth, a wish
for the earth to be solid and not to give,

for concrete or tarmac under the feet,
to rush for the light at the end of the street,

one last race, the utmost desire
to be downing litres of smokeless air

and to run and run and run and run,
and break the finish line, burst a lung.

I watch sirens and lights,
the soldier-ants

of vehicles wearing emergency red
all filing this way.

And people . . . New Yorkers in spate,
a biblical tide flowing north, going safe,

the faces of women and men
looking up at the nightmare of where I am.

Looking back at the monstrous form I've become.
They turn and run.

And through the blitz of that awful snow,
the only colours:

mile beyond mile
of traffic lights changing. Stop. Wait. Go.

12

You have picked me out.
Through a distant shot of a building burning
you have noticed now
that a white cotton shirt is twirling, turning.

In fact I am waving, waving.
Small in the clouds, but waving, waving.
Does anyone see
a soul worth saving?

So when will you come?
Do you think you are watching, watching
a man shaking crumbs
or pegging out washing?

I am trying and trying.
The heat behind me is bullying, driving,
but the white of surrender is not yet flying.
I am not at the point of leaving, diving.

A bird goes by.
The depth is appalling. Appalling
that others like me
should be wind-milling, wheeling, spiralling, falling.

Are your eyes believing,
believing
that here in the gills
I am still breathing.

But tiring, tiring.
Sirens below are wailing, firing.
My arm is numb and my nerves are sagging.
Do you see me, my love. I am failing, flagging.

13

What reveals itself once night has cleared?
What emerges by day,

what fragments, what findings,
what human remains?

The steaming mound like a single corpse:
stony tissue, skeletal steel,

and not matter alone
but ideas as well:

concepts torpedoed
and theories trashed,

refuted schematics,
a carcass of zeroed numbers and graphs.

The gleaners arrive to pick and prise,
to rummage by any and every means:

claw and spike,
hook and crane,

bucket and spade on hands and knees.
Some use the phrase 'a fruitless search',

some fall and weep, some gag and wretch,
some report that death has the scent of a peach.

Neither here
nor there

the will-o-the-wisp of a welder's torch,
two right-angled girders raised as a cross.

The numbers game.
The body count.

All fleshly cargo is stretchered out,
carried by bearers, clothed in flags.

The rest is boated and trucked,
strewn in a field to be raked and forked,

to be sifted and bagged,
numbered and tagged.

What comes to light are the harder things:
eternity rings,

necklaces, bracelets, identity cards,
belt-buckles, cufflinks, ear-rings, combs,

hair-slides, hip-flasks, running shoes,
bones.

Watches are found still keeping time –
the escapement sound, the pulse still alive

but others have locked at ten-twenty-eight.
Others like mine.

And here is a rock from Brighton beach,
here is a beer-mat, here is the leaf

of an oak, pressed and dried, papery thin.
Here is a Liquorice Allsorts tin.

The flag of St George.
A cricket ball.

Here is calendar, counting the days.
Here is a photograph snug in its frame,

this is my wife on our wedding day,
here is a twist of her English hair.

No ashes as such, but cinders and grains
are duly returned,

sieved and spooned and handed back
in a cherry-wood urn in a velvet bag.

All lost.
All lost in the dust.
Lost in the fall and the crush and the dark.
Now all coming back.

Five years on, nothing in place:
the hole in the ground

still an open wound,
the gaps in the sky still empty space,

the scene of the crime still largely the same . . .
but everything changed.

Five years on
what false alarm can be trusted again,
what case or bag can be left unclaimed,
what flight can be sure to steer its course,
what building can claim to own its form,
what column can vow to stand up straight,
what floor can agree to bear its weight,
what tower can vouch to retain its height,
what peace can be said to be water-tight,
what truth can be said to be bullet-proof,
can anything swear to be built to last,
can anything pledge to be hard and fast,
what system can promise to stay in place,
what structure can promise to hold its shape,
what future can promise to keep its faith?

Everything changed. Nothing is safe.

We May Allow Ourselves
a Brief Period of Rejoicing

*

May the 8th 1945.
We were bulldog British and still alive
with the future as bright as the widening sky
in the V of Churchill's victory sign.

Heat in the heart, a lump in the throat,
hope like the sun
and all of us giddy and grateful and young
and we'd won, we'd won, we'd bloody well won.

*

A war that began and ended in rain.
Sprayed bullets of rain.
Rain that drum-rolled
on the church hall roof,
when nice Mr Chamberlain
went to the stage
and fell for the three-card trick
then returned to his seat,
empty handed and deceived.
'I have to tell you now that no such undertaking has been received.'
Empty handed and deceived.
Hard weather ahead. Storms to the east.

The curtains drawn.
A black, underground war.
We kept it dark.
We dug deep,
moved through tunnels and tubes.
We slept in a midnight garden,
in tin sheds
or crypts
of railway sleepers and piled earth.

We dreamed with the worms
under a Braille of stars,
under the ploughed lawns,
under cabbage leaf hats and turnip heads,
under potato roots that dangled down
like severed, uncoupled electrical flex.

Some nights – a blanket silence.
Some nights we woke in sweat
to a sound like a needle or drill coming near,
a nagging, gnawing mosquito drone in the air.
Doodlebugs. Rocketing dinosaur birds . . .

*

'Forty-four, 'forty-five.
A slow surfacing.
Darkness unlocked.

Road-blocks unblocked.
Carved heads
hoisted back on their plinths,

statues dropped into place.
Windows un-taped.
Gas ignited,

a piecemeal sunrise.
A wick
turned gently,

quietly up,
through the night.
Then peace –

what was it like?
Peace like light.
Coal in the hearth.

A bonfire up on the heath.
A ripe, un-rationed tomorrow
of luminous sights,

banana yellow and milk white.

*

Don't speak
to the boy on the bike –
a bullet comes out of his throat.

Don't catch the eye of the boy on the bike –
don't stand in the cross-hairs,
stumble into his line of sight.

Pray if he enters the street,
pray if he leans his bike on the wall,
if he opens the gate.

They say that bike
is little more than a two-wheeled scythe.
They say

in a certain light
you'll notice the skull
just under his skin...

Here he is on the path,
at the window,
cupping his hands to the glass.

Here he is at the door, and you
in a trance, unbolting the bolts,
lifting the latch . . .

In the parlour it's dark.
He steadies himself,
leans on the mantelpiece over the hearth –

look, he's only a boy,
a gangling, pudding-faced, bike-riding youth.
Then he opens his mouth.

*

we're dancing on paving stones
we're scaling the lampposts
we're hitching our skirts
heading up west
we're cheering and leering
from black-eyed windows
streaming from camouflaged
we're picking through splinters
we're out in the terraces
with teapots and doilies
we're singing our hearts out
to tunes rattled out
we're pissing on Wagner
we're hearing the call
to ride on the lions
we're draped on the railings
we're letting off rockets
it's less like VE day
we're off down the alleys
to fondle and fumble
to smother a sailor
we're blowing up condoms
that's half a mile long
and shillies and shallies

till the barrel runs dry

except

for an English oak
and the spangle and spark
in a drunken, one-man
and the dome of St Paul's
still golden and true
the cross on the hill

littered with shrapnel
and mounting the flagpoles
and letting some steam off
for a beer and a knees-up
and waving and leaning
in bomb-struck houses
Anderson shelters
tripping through embers
down on the pavements
on trestles and tables
going bananas
on war-torn Joannas
we're whistling Elgar
so we're off to Trafalgar
and clown in the fountains
at Buckingham Palace
and roman candles
and more like a blitzkrieg
and into the side-streets
with somebody's missus
with lipsticky kisses
we're joining a conga
and wiggles and wanders
and keeps getting longer

and it's almost dark

on fire in the park
of a pearly king
Lambeth Walk
picked out by torch
after years of hell
the cross on the hill

*

Returning from war.
Returning to what?

One man is met.
One man is not.

One man is slapped on the back in the pub.
One man's house is boarded up.

One man's wife takes him straight to bed.
One man's dog comes running. Draws blood.

One man is kissed on the mouth and neck
and the curtains are drawn.

One man sits and stares at the wall.
One man's wife has gone for a walk;

there's a scribbled note,
there's a tin of pilchards under a plate.

One man's wife is flat on her back
with GI Joe doing press-ups on top.

In another man's garden, the flowers and stones
read Welcome Home.

One man weeps in a room on his own.
One man is asked his name by his son.

One man arrives in town at dawn,
can't wait, so gallops

across the meadows and over the moor,
then leaps the gate and sprints the lawn

and opens the door
on a dwindling fire,

and dust in the air,
and his father-in-law asleep in the chair.

*

In the dark Victorian caverns and caves
of Liverpool Street or Charing Cross
we were kissed and combed
and bundled off

on rattling trains
to the vales and shires,
to the end of the line.
So this was the country, the land?

Here we were safe.
After all, what did a tree ever do
to the Hun? What harm was a cow?
Here, the only threat from above

was a pheasant in flight
with its ack-ack call and its flaming tail.
Here in the sticks,
the war was a frogspawn fight, or a kick

from a horse,
or a sabre-toothed rat
in the bog-shed down at the end of the path.
We were aliens. London

was outer space to these bumpkin kids
chewing strands of corn,
off trapping and snaring,
loafing and sneering on five-bar gates.

At dusk, by gaslight, in front of the hearth,
we were mollycoddled
with awkward love,
mothered by maidens and farmers' wives

with kittens for daughters and piglets for sons.
Then at night, from open windows under the thatch,
in the incense of wood-smoke and new-mown grass,
to the oboe playing of sad-faced owls,

we prayed that the clouds wouldn't part,
prayed that the moon wouldn't shine too hard
and open up London like a map,
wouldn't usher bombs towards houses and rooms

where mothers slumbered
and fathers dozed;
parents like ours
dreaming of children like us.

*

(Should we, could we ever go back?
Finger the old wound?
Would the letters and hearts
we gouged in the young bark

have healed over by now?
Or does the rawness still show?
Like some distant, miniscule patch of white,
which after a long hike

turns out to be snow –
one last remaining drift of snow
which has to be touched by human heat
for its ice to weep,

before it can let go.)

*

Those swarms of planes
under cover of clouds
with their thunder bolts
and terror blows
couldn't dint St Paul's
and its bull's eye dome.
We scanned the sky,
and some will say
they spotted one day
some mark or fleck
like dirt in the eye

which suddenly mushroomed
and slowed and swung
and drifted down
on silk and strings,
not an object or thing
but a human, a man.

One of theirs.
One of them.

*

The stars took the shape of a Swastika once
but the heavenly bodies are ordered back.
Now there's a V sign, a spitfire, a Union Jack.

Last year there were Nazis at work
in the sewers and drains, a wolf in the wardrobe,
a storm-trooper under the bed. Last week

the cellar was Auschwitz, the attic was Belsen,
the bath tub was beached in the shallows at Dunkirk,
the barbed wire fence at the end of the lane

was the limit – the front-line.
Today there's an apple, a smug-looking egg teed up in a cup,
the promise of meat, a trout to be cooked.

Like Eden again. Britannia back on her throne.
But it's quiet. It's small.
If war is an illness overcome

then here is the patient partly restored –
a nation in convalescence,
confined to quarters, better, but… bored.

Because after the glamour of tanks and guns
come the pots and the pans.
The errands, the jobs and the chores.

And after the vigour of war – its body and soul –
come the nuts and the bolts, the pillows and pennies
and dishes and buttons and clothes.

Hands which braided the brigadier's cap,
or primed grenades
with a trembling pin,

hands which shook with the effort of war
or whetted the bayonet knife
or folded and tucked the parachute packs

now turn to a life less famous, less keen:
to the point of a pen, to the bluntness of bread
and the making of beds.

The show is over.
Garlands rain on an empty stage.
After Churchill, actors seem fake or lame.

Not that war doesn't leave its mark:
sixty years after the doodlebug's drone
we flinch or shrink from the dentist's drill

and the lawnmower's buzz;
we dance to the doodlebug's tune. And sixty years on
we throw back the curtains and muse

on the wrought iron railings and garden gates
refashioned as bullets or shells.
And we stare in to space.

We were saved, all saved for good, and utterly changed –
agreed. But there, at the time,
on the winning side of the finishing line,

in the glare of unconditional light,
in the litter of glory,
and after the beer and the flags

and triumphant dancing and mad, jubilant sex,
we stood for a while, and waited, waited,
wondering what came next.

Cambodia

1)

Is evil a substance, a thing?
Does it wait?
Does it seethe?
Does it grow?
Does it breed?

Does it demonstrate cycles of life,
pass through a larval stage,
does it lie cocooned, growing eyes and wings?

Does evil snooze in a hammock slung between trees?

Does evil germinate, radiate, rise?
Does it bloom under money and power?
Does it seep like gas through keyholes
and under the doors of the poor?

Cambodia. Say it. A word.

A bowl of rice peppered with red corn.
A brilliant mind ordered to carry dirt.
Monday – carrying dirt.
Tuesday – carrying dirt.
Winter – carrying dirt.
Five years transplanting seedlings of rice, shoot by shoot,
barrowing dung,
carrying dirt
under the butt of a gun, under the eye of boy.

A Buddhist monk smashed with a spade and lashed to a tree.
A young man smashed for saying the wrong word.

Survive. Hide in a hole sucking sugar sap out of the raw cane.

Can evil be touched?
Does evil itself touch?
The tap on the shoulder, the rap on the door after dark.
The firm hand on the elbow. 'Come this way.'

Can evil be buried?
Can evil be ground down, bulldozed into a pit and left to rot?
Does it sweat?
Year on year will it decompose, each half-life decaying, passing away,
ticking down till extinct.

Or ploughed back, will it surface again?
Will it elbow out of the mud in the clawing rain?
Will its femurs and jaw-bones sprout and shoot,

will the seeds of its marrow take root?
In an unmarked field will evil, left to itself, lift its finger again one day,
rise through the earth, stare from its empty eyes?

Cambodia. Say it. A word.

A room.
Leg-irons hung from a nail on a wall in a room.
Jump leads. A blindfold. Crocodile clips.
The teeth of a hacksaw pitted with dried blood.

An idea gone bad?
A theory afloat in the water, underside up.
A clean start, perfect and pure, like milk straight from the goat,
but left in the sun for too long.
A rancid, diseased thought.

And whose brainchild or birthstone was this?
What is it, this rouge?
Why red – is it fire, is it blood?

Zero the clock.
Start with the youth.
Red in the schools,
the children all thinking red, all brainwashed with red,
red in their tongues and their nerves and their nostrils and eyes and ears,
learning by red rote,
adding their red sums,
planting their red rice,
drinking their red milk.
Wearing their black clothes.

The daughter who left. No word. Came back in a year to collect a spade.
The son who left. No word. Came back with a pistol hooked in his belt.
The brother who joined up. No word. His bicycle found in a ditch.
No word from the family of twelve loaded into a truck.
No word from the man who was singled out,
a husband who chose as his final meal
a modest portion of chicken and rice
to share with his wife,
but even before the wishbone cracked
boy-soldiers in black
were easing their way through eggplant bushes, approaching the house.
With the snout of his gun, a boy-soldier raises the hasp of the gate.

Red shadows. Shadows of rouge.

Names on a list.
Your name on a list – the call of death.
Fear of a name – your own.

Your name called out.
Your name in somebody's mouth. Out loud. Kneel down.

The pop of a gun behind a hut.
A million faces defaced, face down in the dirt.

Why here?
Why then?

Were conditions ripe?
Did it hatch from an egg?
Did it blow in on the breeze?
Did it ooze through a crack in the earth?
Did somebody find it asleep under a stone, poke it awake it with stick?
Did it spring from a little red book like a jack-in-a-box?
Was it good gone wrong?
Is evil a thing – does is sleep, lie dormant, hibernate, waken, emerge . . .

Cambodia. Say it. A word,

still spitting its teeth
still tilling its bones
still bearing its scars
still wearing its rags
still hunting its cause
still haunting its fields
still ringing its hands
still singing its wars
still darning its holes
still reading its stars
still hiding its eyes
still finding its dead
still fighting its ghost

still tending its grave
still trimming its shrine
still pointing its blame
still swabbing its stain
still piling its skulls
still pinning its hope
still nursing its wound
still letting its blood

11)

What is good?

Does it leaf?
Does it fruit or bloom?
Does it hold at its centre some nut or kernel or stone of truth?

Will good come about on its own?
Left to itself, will it pool like stream-water, scooping a bowl in the rock.

Good – is it a human thought?
Are its knuckles tattooed with the letters of love?
Does the bird know of good,
does the snake,
the river,
the kettle,
the rain?

Is it something to do with the phase of the moon or the pattern of stars?
Is good on first-name terms with fate?

Or is goodness learned?
Or is goodness earned – desired and deserved?
Or is good like the moth which ghosted itself through the prison
     bars
and set itself down on the skin of a man
who had not eaten in nineteen days
but who felt the touch of its weightless weight on his boneless
     bones,
and saw it as hope?

This man or the next,
bludgeoned for wearing glasses to read,
or the next,
bludgeoned for stealing a rodent to eat,
or the next,
bludgeoned for falling asleep on his feet,
or the next,
bludgeoned for having a thought in his head,
then bludgeoned again
then bludgeoned again.

Is good in the nature of man?
Is there a God named Good?

Can goodness be bartered for, swapped for a dog,
drawn from the well or yanked from the lake?

Auto-genocide – the given term.
Say it. A word.

A jail without walls.

At night, music blares from the speakers

to cover the screams.
Cambodia staying alive by plying the guards with wine.
Cambodia staying alive by eating its lice and fleas.
Cambodia witnessing line after line after line after line after line
    of Cambodians
clubbed on the back of the skull by Cambodians
slashing the throats of Cambodians
swords in the hands of Cambodians
blood in the eyes of Cambodians
blood from the ears of Cambodians
dragging the dead of Cambodia smashed by Cambodians
into a pit of Cambodians many Cambodians deep...

A Cambodian killed for touching the hand of his son
A Cambodian killed for talking aloud in his sleep
A Cambodian killed for dropping a spoon in a dish

Cambodian telling Cambodian
you – your life is no profit, your death is no loss.
Cambodian smashing Cambodian literally into the dirt,
not shot but hammered to death because bullets are money –
bullets have physical worth.

A year, then the next, then the next, then the next, then the next.

Then a day like the last, a morning, a bell rings,
a bell rings it's morning it's over it's finished it's done.

You can go home.

To where? To what?

Can the mind be a map

rolled out, rolled up, redrawn overnight?
Or is it a country, a place,
a living land in its own right:
thick jungle, high summits, slow rivers, wide planes,
and memory
an obstinate buffalo up to its flanks in a swamp,
a sharp-headed raptor soaring between peaks,
a dark blue lizard snug in the cracks of Angkor Wat,
a slow, shadowy fish passing under the boat. . .

Cambodia. Say it. A word.

A space in the jungle cleared of its ferns and wood.
Pol Pot lying dead, as dead as a man, in a small hut.

Grey flannels, pink flowers,
a short-sleeved shirt.
A lime green coverlet shrouding his feet.
The eyes drawn shut.

That his heart had stopped. That he didn't wake up.

A makeshift, bric-à-brac funeral pyre:
a soiled mattress, a wicker chair, a patterned blanket, a bald tyre.
The blur of fire.
A photograph – easily done.

Will goodness arrive but that which is worked at and hard won?

When will the dark come clean?
When will blame enter the dock?
When will today, washed of its camouflage paint, look itself in the face?

Like the last boy-soldiers deep in the forests and groves,
when will guilt emerge from beneath the cover of trees,
gun pointing down,
eyes forward,
palms up?